chow chow

pug

dachshund

schnauzer

chinese crested

german shepherd

saint bernard

chow
chow

pug

dachshund

schnauzer

chinese
crested

german shepherd

saint bernard

Dog Poems

Dave Crawley

Illustrations by Tamara Petrosino

Wordsong

HONESDALE, PENNSYLVANIA

To Laurel and Dixon, the golden-hearted retrievers, and the loyal service dogs at the Assistance Dog Institute of Santa Rosa, California
—D.C.

To the memory of Daisy, the best little dog ever; and to Zombie, who's as big as a dog; and to Phantom and Charles, who play fetch like a dog, with love
—T.P.

Text copyright © 2007 by Dave Crawley
Illustrations copyright © 2007 by Tamara Petrosino
All rights reserved

Wordsong
An Imprint of Boyds Mills Press, Inc.
815 Church Street
Honesdale, Pennsylvania 18431
Printed in China

Library of Congress Cataloging-in-Publication Data

Crawley, Dave.
  Dog poems / by Dave Crawley ; illustrations by Tamara Petrosino. — 1st ed.
    p. cm.
  ISBN-13: 978-1-59078-454-9 (alk. paper)
  1. Dogs—Juvenile poetry. 2. Dog owners—Juvenile poetry. 3. Children's poetry, American. I. Petrosino, Tamara, ill. II. Title.

PS3603.R399D64 2007
811'.6—dc22

2006038104

First edition, 2007
The text of this book is set in 14-point New Times Roman.
The illustrations are done in pen and ink and watercolor.

10 9 8 7 6 5 4 3 2 1

Contents

OODLES OF POODLES

Oodles of poodles
strut through the park.
They come in the morning
and just before dark.

Poodles in pigtails.
Poodles in skirts.
Poodles with pompoms
and little pink shirts.

White poodles. Black poodles.
Caramel-coated.
Big ones that trot
and toys that are toted.

Caboodles of poodles.
A poodle convention!
Yet nobody barks.
No poodle dissension.

Good poodles are proper,
and that's only right.
A courteous poodle
is always poo-lite.

BASSET

The saggy baggy Basset hound
has ears that nearly touch the ground,
with mournful eyes and wrinkled skin
that hangs below his droopy chin.

But Basset has a clever snout.
His nose will always sniff you out.
With this amazing nasal asset,
nothing can get past the Basset.

SOGGY DOGGY

Spittery-splottery-spluttery-splat!
A very good day for owning a cat.
But I have a dog, who pulls on his chain,
enjoying our slippery slog in the rain.

We're finally home! It's cozy and dry.
I take off my raincoat and let out a sigh.
I'm starting to sneeze, beginning to cough.
He chooses this moment to shake himself off.

Big globules of water cascade through the air.
I'm showered! I'm soaked! From my toes to my hair!
He's splashing the furniture! Drenching the rug!
Now he comes over expecting a hug!

Spittery-splottery-spluttery-splat!
A very good day for owning a cat.

SHAGGY SHEEPDOG

Shaggy sheepdog on a rock
guards the grazing woolly flock.
So much fur, there's just no trace
of the shaggy sheepdog's face.
Wide awake or fast asleep?
Either way, she's counting sheep.

8

MOONDOG

Sea gulls take flight as she bounds through the surf,
unleashing a fountain of spray.
When the sun disappears, the beach is her turf.
She rules at the end of the day.

In the shimmery glimmery glow of the moon,
she splashes up crystals of light.
A shadowy shape on the crest of a dune,
she howls with the salt winds of night.

At sunrise, when hikers return to this land,
and wave-seeking surfers appear,
only her paw prints, embedded in sand,
reveal that the Moondog was here.

YIP-YIP WOOF!

Tiny Chihuahua.
Humongous Great Dane.
The difference between them
is really quite plain.

Feisty Chihuahua
will yap-yap and yip.
If he doesn't like you,
you may get a nip!

Gentle Great Dane
has a powerful bite
but never would nip you.
She's much too polite.

Great Dane finds the carpet
a fine place to nap.
Chihuahua loves curling
right up in your lap.

Their owners would have
some cause for dismay
if each dog behaved
in the opposite way.

LAZY OLD MAZY

Lazy old Mazy, asleep in the sun,
can't see any reason to jump up and run.
Lackadaisically hazy,
she sprawls on the lawn,
slothfully, sluggishly,
listlessly, luggishly,
wearily, blearily,
eyes drooping drearily,
waking up only to yawn.

But Mazy is not what she seems.

In truth, she's a fighter,
a biter of bears,
protector of children,
and chaser of hares.
With feats of agility,
Mazy's ability
wins her blue ribbons at fairs.

But only, of course, in her dreams.

12

SNUGGLE-WUGGLE

When I am in
a huggy mood,
and you are in
a snuggy mood,
we love to snuggle-wuggle
on the rug.

Your fur will
ruzzle-wuzzle me.
And if you'd like
to nuzzle me,
I'll happily repay you
with a hug!

13

WOLF DOG

At the edge of a wood, in a world long ago,
a hunter cooks meat on a fire.
Piercing the darkness, a pair of eyes glow.
They watch with a hungry desire.

Aware of the wolf who is watching him eat,
a hunter is willing to share.
He tosses a bone of savory meat.
The wolf takes it back to her lair.

She comes once again on the following night
to the edge of the smoke-covered haze.
She creeps a bit closer, in spite of her fright,
to the warmth of the flickering blaze.

The man and the wolf are together at last,
with a trust that grows deeper each day.
How many thousands of years have gone past
since that hunter convinced her to stay?

A man lights a fire as his dog curls up tight,
fatigued from a romp in the snow.
She dreams of a wolf who emerged from the night
on the edge of a wood, long ago.

SNOWBALL

I found a lost puppy one dark snowy night.
Her eyes were pitch-black, but her coat was pure white.
Snowball I called her. It suited her fine.
When nobody claimed her, I knew she was mine.

A couple days later, I spotted a spot.
A mark on her forehead. A tiny black dot.
I rubbed and I scrubbed. It would not go away.
Then more spots appeared on the following day.

"Is it measles?" I wondered while calling the vet.
He laughed and advised me to rename my pet.
I'd made the wrong choice for a puppy so spotty.
My Snowball is now a Dalmatian named Dotty.

ADOPTING GRACIE

Gracie the greyhound was not very fast.
She never did well at the track.
But I didn't care if she always ran last,
alone at the back of the pack.

Gracie the greyhound was not very fast,
but that doesn't matter to me.
As we walk down the path, we don't think of the past,
'cause Gracie the greyhound is free.

ALMOST HUMAN

We take them to groomers.
We fumble and fuss
to make our poor dogs
behave just like us.

"My dog's nearly human!"
We say it with pride.
But how many canines
have gossiped or lied?

How many dogs
would mock us or tease us?
Dogs have one goal
and that is to please us.

They give us devotion
and never condemn.
Perhaps we should act
a bit more like them.

18

WASHING THE DOG

She dives in the river.
She swims in the lake.

She celebrates snow
from the very first flake.

She plunges through puddles
that lie in her path.
My puppy loves water
(except in a bath).

I tried with a washtub.
I sprayed with a hose.

But most of the water
went right up my nose.

And when we were done,
it was easy to see,
the only one getting a shower was me!

OUCH!

Hark!
Bark!
Tail!
Flail!
Swipe!
Yipe!
Arp!
Sharp!
Yelp!
Help!

This poem needs just one more line:
don't ever chase a porcupine.

NO BEAUTIFUL BULLDOGS

You won't find a beautiful bulldog,
no matter how hard you may try.
With a low-hanging jowl
and a permanent scowl,
he isn't a glamorous guy.

His head is too big for his body.
His body is shaped like a pear.
He's stubby and lumpy
and always looks grumpy.
But such a description's unfair.

Bulldogs aren't meant to be lovely.
They're not meant to scamper and leap.
They're loyal and gentle.
So it's fundamental
that beauty is only fur deep.

I BOUGHT MY DOG A CELL PHONE

I bought my dog a cell phone.
I didn't mind the cost.
I figured I could call him
whenever he got lost.

Woof!

Bow-wow-Wow!

But when I dialed his number
and asked, "Where are you now?"
his answers were not helpful:
just *Woof!* and *Bow-wow-wow!*

DOG BED

We bought a new dog bed for Woofer to use.
A snug bed. A rug bed. Just right for a snooze.
There's a little dog pillow for resting his head
(since Woofer's too big now for sharing my bed).
He's curled in the corner, not making a peep.
I'll fluff up my pillow and drift off to . . . *Yeep!*

Ow! Yow!
Ouch! Youch!
Yelp! Help!
Bow! Wow!

Get off my feet!
Give back my sheet!
Don't lick my face!
I need more space!

I reach for my blanket and fall to the floor,
while up in my bed he's beginning to snore.
That's not how I planned it, but that's how it is.
The dog bed is my bed, and my bed is his!

TELLING A TAIL

A happy tail wags.

A gloomy tail sags.

A frightened tail tucks
under hind legs and drags.

Your puppy's emotions
come through, without fail.

Whatever he's feeling,
his tail tells a tale.

THE LABRADOR LOVES LIQUID

The Labrador loves liquid
(I don't mean just to drink).
He'll splash through flowing streamlets
and sticky bogs that stink.

With devotion to the ocean,
he thunders through the spray.
The sea is grand for swimming,
and surf is meant for play.

He'll stand beneath a rain flood
cascading from the roof.
The water rolls right off him,
since Labs are waterproof.

JUNKYARD DOG

The junkyard dog
won't yap
or yip.
He never even
howls.
But don't go near.
There's cause to fear
that rumble-grumble
sound you hear.
He doesn't bark.
He growwwls!

PEKINGESE

The Pekingese
is quite Chinese.
They named him for Peking.
But now that town
of great renown
goes by the name *Beijing*.

His name should change.
Let's rearrange
the letters, if you please.
Good-bye, Peking.
Hello, Beijing.
We'll call him *Beijingese*.

WRONG KITTY

Bartholomew chased the wrong kitty,
which helps to explain why he stunk.
We can't let him in. It's a pity.
The "kitty" he chased was a skunk.

SLOBBERKISS

A kiss on the lips? A smack on the cheek?
Would a peck on the nose do the trick?
A slobbery smooch from my passionate pooch
can cover all three in a lick!

THE WELL-WORN PATH

You scampered down this well-worn path
when you were just a pup.
And as we grew, I ran with you.
I struggled to keep up.

My legs grew long. Your legs grew slow.
You're happy now to walk,
ignoring all those squirrels and birds
you once would chase and stalk.

And as we walk I think of all
the moments that we shared.
The day we found you at the pound,
you looked so small and scared.

The times I fed you table scraps
in spite of Mother's rule.

The days you greeted me with joy
when I came home from school.

And as we walk this well-worn path,
no longer running free,
I hope I was as good to you
as you have been to me.

chow chow

pug

dachshund

schnauzer

chinese crested

saint bernard

german shepherd

chow
chow

pug

dachshund

schnauzer

chinese
crested

german shepherd

saint bernard